Crayola

CRAYOLA
SCIENCE
OF
COLOR

Mari Schuh

Lerner Publications ◆ Minneapolis

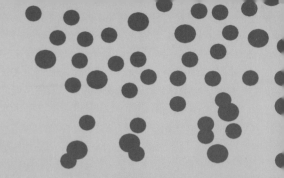

TO LILLIANA, HEZEKIAH, CORA, AND ADDIE

Official Licensed Product
Lerner Publications Company
A division of Lerner Publishing Group, Inc.
241 First Avenue North
Minneapolis, MN 55401 USA

For reading levels and more information, look up this title at www.lernerbooks.com.

Main body text set in Billy Infant Regular 24/40.
Typeface provided by SparkyType.

Library of Congress Cataloging-in-Publication Data

Names: Schuh, Mari C., 1975–
Title: Crayola science of color / by Mari Schuh.
Description: Minneapolis : Lerner Publications, [2018] | Series: Crayola colorology | Audience: Age 4–9. | Audience: K to grade 3. | Includes bibliographical references and index.
Identifiers: LCCN 2017019012 (print) | LCCN 2017016629 (ebook) | ISBN 9781512497755 (eb pdf) | ISBN 9781512466911 (lb : alk. paper) | ISBN 9781541511651 (pb : alk. paper)
Subjects: LCSH: Color—Juvenile literature. | Light—Juvenile literature. | Crayons—Juvenile literature.
Classification: LCC QC495.5 (print) | LCC QC495.5 .S3687 2018 (ebook) | DDC 535.6—dc23

LC record available at https://lccn.loc.gov/2017016629

Manufactured in the United States of America
1-43082-32456-7/7/2017

TABLE OF CONTENTS

COLOR ALL AROUND

We see colors all around us.

Color is everywhere!

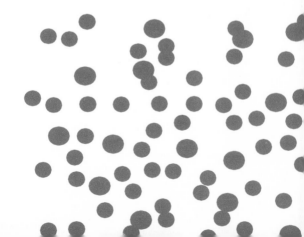

5

WHAT IS COLOR?

We see color because of light.

Light lets us see all the colors of a rainbow.

Sunlight shines through raindrops to make a rainbow.

Green, blue, yellow, and red. Everything we see has a color!

Light bounces off materials so we can see them.

Green light bounces off a green shirt.
Yellow light bounces off a yellow shirt.

Eyes have tiny parts called cones.

Cones help us see colors.

Light touches the cones.

The cones tell our brains what colors we see.

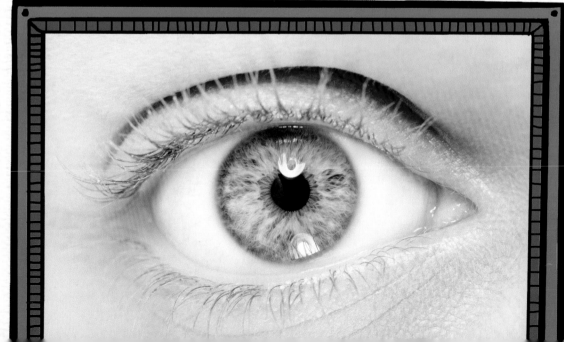

COLORS TOGETHER

Colors work together!

Some colors mix to make other colors.

Some colors help other colors stand out.

Yellow, red, and blue are called primary colors.

Primary colors can't be made from other colors.

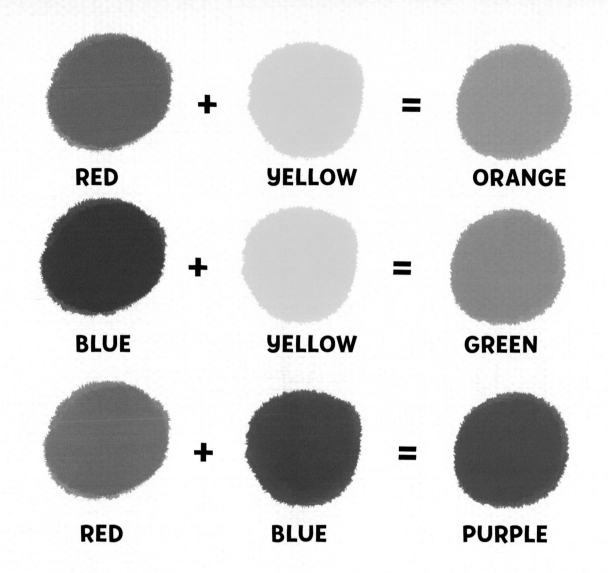

RED + YELLOW = ORANGE

BLUE + YELLOW = GREEN

RED + BLUE = PURPLE

Orange, green, and purple are secondary colors.

They are made by mixing two primary colors.

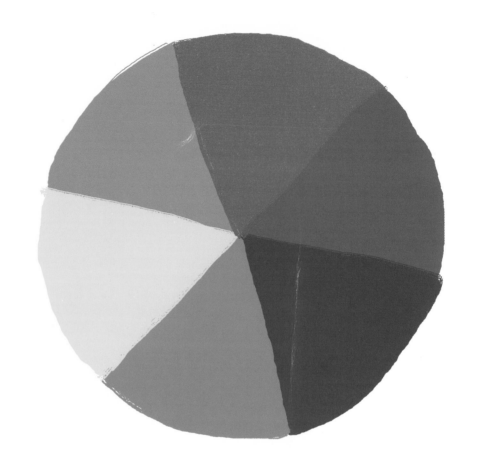

A color wheel shows us how colors are related.

Complementary colors are opposites on the color wheel.

Purple and yellow are complementary colors.
They are bold and easy to see!

Red, orange, and yellow are warm colors.

They remind us of the sun.

Blue, green, and purple are cool colors.

They remind us of water and the sky.

COLORS IN THE WORLD

We learn more about color all the time!

Scientists made a new bright blue pigment—by accident!

They called it YlnMn blue for the chemicals it is made of.

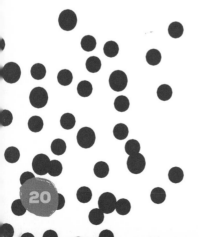

Colors look different with different colors around them.

Which red box looks the brightest?

23

Sometimes colors stand out.

Sometimes colors blend in.

Can you find the insect hiding in the fall leaves?

Colors can make us calm.

They can also give us energy!

What colors do you like best?

MANY COLORS

The world is filled with so many colors.

Find these Crayola® colors in the photos.

Purple Heart

Goldenrod

Mango Tango

Granny Smith Apple

Cerise

Outrageous Orange

Brick Red

Turquoise

GLOSSARY

color wheel: a diagram that shows how colors are related

complementary colors: colors that are opposites on the color wheel

cones: special cells in the eye that sense colored light

pigment: a substance that gives color to other materials such as paint, plastic, or fabric

primary colors: colors that can't be made from other colors. Red, yellow, and blue are primary colors.

secondary colors: colors that are made by mixing two primary colors. Orange, green, and purple are secondary colors.

TO LEARN MORE

BOOKS

Blevins, Wiley. *Colors All Around*. South Egremont, MA: Red Chair, 2016.
　　Read about a young girl discovering all the colors around her.

Osburn, Mary Rose. *I Know Colors*. New York: Gareth Stevens, 2017.
　　Explore color by reading about common objects you might see every day.

Schuh, Mari. *Crayola Art of Color*. Minneapolis: Lerner Publications, 2018.
　　Learn about color by studying famous works of art.

WEBSITES

The Color Wheel
　　http://www.kidzone.ws/science/colorwheel.htm
　　Read more about the color wheel.

Explore Color
　　http://www.crayola.com/explore-colors
　　Learn all about color through coloring pages and color experiments.

Light and Color
　　http://pbskids.org/dragonflytv/show/lightandcolor.html
　　Find out more about light and color.

INDEX

PHOTO ACKNOWLEDGMENTS

The images in this book are used with the permission of: © RoyStudioEU/Shutterstock.com (linen background throughout); © Lisa F. Young/Dreamstime.com, p. 5 (left); © Ashifa R./Dreamstime.com, p. 5 (top right); © Alain Lacroix/Dreamstime.com, p. 5 (bottom right); © GODONG/Science Source, p. 7; © Michael Flippo/Dreamstime.com, p. 9; iStock.com/Freder, p. 11 (top); iStock.com/stock_colors, p. 11 (bottom); iStock.com/konradlew, p. 13 (top left); iStock.com/nevodka, p. 13 (bottom left); iStock.com/Syldavia, p. 13 (top right); iStock.com/CathyKeifer, p. 13 (bottom right); iStock.com/SumikoPhoto, p. 13 (center); © Rosenfeld Images Ltd/Science Source, p. 14; Action Plus Sports Images/Alamy Stock Photo, p. 17; © maxime raynal/flickr.com (CC BY 2.0), p. 18; © Christian Araujo/Dreamstime. com, p. 19; Mas Subramanian/Wikimedia Commons (CC BY-SA 4.0), p. 21; © Thomas Marent/Minden Pictures, p. 25; iStock.com/YuriyS, p. 27 (top); iStock.com/SolStock, p. 27 (bottom); Brian T. Evans/Moment/Getty Images, p. 28.

Cover: © Anna Om/Dreamstime.com (sunset); LiskaM/Shutterstock.com (balloons); © Nila Newsom/Dreamstime.com (colored dyes); bogdan ionescu/Shutterstock.com (rainbow); RoyStudioEU/Shutterstock.com (linen texture background); TairA/Shutterstock.com (watercolor background).

LERNER
SOURCE™

Expand learning beyond the printed book. Download free, complementary educational resources for this book from our website, www.lerneresource.com.